Introduction

This book is a photographic survey of the ever-changing bus scene in north-west England. The book in effect covers the historic county of Lancashire, which was considerably altered from 1 April 1974.

Historically, Lancashire stretched from the Furness Fells and Cartmel Peninsula on the boundary with Cumberland and Westmorland respectively, and thence down to the River Mersey, which forms the historic boundary with Cheshire. The hilly east side of Lancashire was bounded by the West Riding of Yorkshire and the coastal plain with the Irish Sea. Lancashire was a late entry on the English county map, being created as late as 1182. Lancaster was traditionally the county town, a position now held by Preston. The city of Preston is situated on the north bank of the Ribble, a river that effectively divides Lancashire in two. The area north of Preston is more rural in character and far less industrialised than the south and east. The Cartmel and Furness regions were severed from Lancashire in 1974, becoming part of the artificial county of Cumbria. Many people are surprised to learn that Cartmel, Coniston, Grange-over-Sands, Torver, and Ulverston are Lancastrian towns, sometimes known as Lancashire-over-the-Sands or North Lonsdale. Cumbria County Council is set to be abolished in 2023, with the Lancashire parts forming a new unitary authority called Westmorland and Furness Council.

Today north Lancashire covers the city of Lancaster (Carnforth, Lancaster, Morecambe, and the Lune Valley), the Wyre district and the Ribble Valley. The latter district includes the Forest of Bowland, plus Bolton-by-Bowland, Gisburn, and Sawley, gained from Yorkshire in 1974.

East Lancashire is still suffering from post-war industrial decline. Districts such as Burnley, Hyndburn, Rossendale, and Pendle combine impressive Pennine scenery with numerous small towns, canals, mills, and other traces of the Industrial Revolution. The larger towns including Accrington, Blackburn, and Nelson are racially and socially diverse, and have some economic problems and deprivation. A policy institute in the 2000s suggested allowing places like Blackburn to be allowed to decline naturally and depopulate over time. Can you imagine the uproar if 'managed decline' was proposed for places like Camberley, Gravesend, Hastings, Luton, Sheerness, and Woking?

Preston stands proudly on the River Ribble and beside the M6 – the first stretch of English motorway. A city since 2002, Preston is a significant regional centre with a broad mix of architectural styles, a diverse population, and a large university. Since 1974, the city has included the previously independent and prosperous district of Fulwood.

West of Preston is the area known as the Fylde. A flat plain, the Fylde has a largely rural character until one reaches the coast. Here the contrasting seaside towns of Fleetwood, Thornton-Cleveleys, Blackpool, and Lytham St Annes act as a magnet for tourists and form a significant percentage of Lancashire's population total.

South of Preston are the districts of Chorley, South Ribble, and West Lancashire. South Ribble is to some degree Greater Preston, and contains the Central Lancashire New Town based on Leyland, plus Bamber Bridge and villages such as Samlesbury to the east. West Lancashire is rural in character but has two contrasting settlements: the new town of Skelmersdale and the more traditional market town of Ormskirk. It is worth noting that Blackburn with Darwen and Blackpool are unitary authorities and no longer officially part of Lancashire.

The bulk of historic Lancashire's population now reside in the former metropolitan counties of Greater Manchester and Merseyside. Both counties were formed in 1974 and include significant portions of historic Cheshire.

Greater Manchester's Lancashire portions include the boroughs of Bolton, Bury, Manchester, Rochdale, Salford, and Wigan. Oldham annexed Saddleworth from Yorkshire, while Tameside and Trafford gained territory from both Lancashire and Cheshire in 1974. There was also a plan to include Wilmslow within Greater Manchester, but after much opposition the affluent commuter town remained in Cheshire, part of the enlarged Macclesfield district, until April 2009.

Merseyside is in the main formed from Lancashire, and includes Southport, which is further north than Ormskirk. Lancashire in Merseyside is comprised of the boroughs of Knowsley, Liverpool, Sefton, and St Helens. Wirral is Cheshire, while St Helens, especially around Haydock and Newton-le-Willows, is said to have very little infinity with Liverpool-dominated Merseyside. In March 2022, the *Liverpool Echo* reported the desire of Southport and Ainsdale to cede from Sefton and join West Lancashire Borough Council. The proposal was supported by the MPs of both Southport and West Lancashire.

Two more areas covered in this book are Halton and Warrington. Situated between Liverpool and Manchester, these unitary authorities have something of an identity crisis. Both boroughs were placed into Cheshire in 1974 and became self-governing in 1998. Warrington is mainly Lancashire, with the exception of suburbs such as Grappenhall, Stockton Heath, and Stretton, which lie south of the Manchester Ship Canal. Halton is effectively Runcorn and Widnes, the latter a proud Lancashire community. The pretty canalside village of Moore is pure Cheshire; Hale and Hale Bank, on the other hand, are pure Lancashire.

So sit back and enjoy a photographic journey of buses around historic Lancashire, taken mainly in 2021–22. As can be expected it is difficult to include all the urban areas of northern England. Some places I have never visited, such as Southport, while others I never seem to have a camera on me – Denton, Formby, and Standish. So apologies to Abram, Chorley, Huyton, Moston, Swinton and elsewhere for missing you out. On the other hand, this book does include somewhat underrepresented places such as Farnworth, Golborne, Halewood, Moss Side, Padiham, and Rishton.

Buses in Lancashire, Greater Manchester and Merseyside is not a book about bus types, engines and companies per se, rather it is a visual and historic record for future generations. Many of the pictures attempt to show buses in their environment, including bus stations, key arterial routes, or suburbs.

The book will be interesting to return to in several decades time – or so I hope! Those who would like to know more about buses themselves and bus operators are recommended to read the excellent *Bus Handbook* series or the various bus magazines such as *Buses*. There are also numerous websites, and of course the PSV Circle.

I would like to thank like to thank Thomas Anthony for proofreading the text. All photographs are by the author unless otherwise stated. Finally, any errors in this book are mine.

A Stagecoach driver training bus at Failsworth, Greater Manchester, on 12 November 2021.

Stagecoach No. 15852 at Walton-le-Dale in the South Ribble district of Lancashire.

As a concession to those who mourn the loss of Lancashire-over-the-Sands to Cumbria in 1974, the first selection of pictures takes a slight liberty with the title of this publication. Service 5 operates from Barrow-in-Furness Town Hall to Walney Island. On 27 January 2022, the route was unusually being worked by an ADL Enviro400-bodied Scania N230UD. No. 15728 passes The Crown at North Scale on a route usually worked by Optare Solos.

Traversing Moor Lane, Flookburgh, towards Haven Lakeland Holiday Park, is this Mercedes-Benz Sprinter used by Mountain Goat. Flookburgh is a former fishing village that never quite progressed to town status. Granted a market charter at some point in the eleventh century, the village has a square and one residential building dating from 1686, plus the slightly detached Ravenstown settlement, built during the First World War to serve an airship station – now Cark Airfield. Flookburgh, 20 May 2022.

Wright StreetLite RX61 DEE is frequently used by The Travellers Choice on service 530 between Kendal and Cartmel. A rather ungainly looking bus, it was pictured at Church Road, Allithwaite, on the last part of the journey to Cartmel. Allithwaite is a good starting point for hikes to Humphrey Head and Hampsfell, although bus services in the village are limited to one journey to Kendal and back. Allithwaite, 15 February 2022.

The Optare Solo is used for a wide variety of bus services due to its reliability, spacious interior, and versatility. As happy in Lancaster as in rural Lancashire, Stagecoach No. 47964 was photographed at Yealand Redmayne, a trim village between Carnforth and Silverdale. Leighton Moss, the largest reed bed in north-west England, is situated near the village.

Optare Solo No. 47964 again, in the delightful surroundings of Yealand Conyers. Pevsner called the village street 'exceptionally pleasant'. Interesting buildings to note are the Friends Meeting House of 1692 and Leighton Hall, once home to Lancaster's famous cabinetmaker R. Gillow.

North Lancashire has numerous pretty villages located within easy reach of Lancaster and the M6. At Over Kellet, famous for its stone crosses, Stagecoach No. 27744 works towards Carnforth and Warton on service 49 from Lancaster. The house on the right, at Kellet Road, is dated 1704. Over Kellet, 23 September 2021.

An unidentified Stagecoach Enviro400 approaches the bus stop at Market Street, Carnforth, on a drab 1 May 2021. The Haematite Iron Company and railways turned Carnforth into a small town in Victorian times. Pevsner warned potential visitors to Carnforth in 1969: 'Apart from the church there is nothing one would seek out.' Harsh words indeed from a man known for pulling no punches.

In north Lancashire, the M6 takes most of the heavy traffic, which once burdened the A6 between Carnforth and Lancaster. Stagecoach No. 12209 calls at Main Road, Bolton-le-Sands on a morning rush hour departure to lonely Overton. 17 February 2022.

Hest Bank is famous as the start, or end point, of the passage across Morecambe Bay to Kents Bank (Grange-over-Sands). The sands are notoriously tricky and an expert guide is essential for safe navigation. Before the arrival of the railway, numerous stagecoaches were caught by the tides attempting to reach Grange or Ulverston (via Flookburgh). A solitary pensioner prepares to board Stagecoach No. 11153 for the safe journey to Lancaster on 7 March 2022.

The area to the east of Lancaster known as the Lune Valley comprises a number of suburbanised villages (Halton and Caton), plus charming settlements such as Hornby and Melling. One of Lancaster districts prettiest spots is Crook o' Lune, near Caton. Stagecoach ADL Enviro300 No. 27753 approaches Caton Lune Bridge on a crisp 7 March 2022, bound for Ingleton, North Yorkshire.

An interesting sight between Lancaster and Hornby is the Claughton Brick Works. Stagecoach No. 22609 passes under the aerial ropeway on a damp 21 August 2021. The works is out of view on the right, close to the River Lune. The conveyor feeds the works with clay from Claughton Moor, a prominence that can be seen for miles around.

On 24 April 2021, Stagecoach No. 10556 crosses Skerton Bridge, Lancaster. Resplendent in The Lakes Connection branding, it has worked the long but scenic route from Keswick to Lancaster. Skerton Bridge was constructed between 1783 and 1788, and leads to a tortuous one-way system around the congested city centre. Lancaster is the traditional county town of Lancashire, a function now performed by Preston.

The quayside area of Lancaster, known as Marsh, has seen considerable regeneration and gentrification in recent years. Stagecoach No. 22598 carries the latest corporate livery as it passes under the railway viaduct at St George's Quay, Lancaster. Out of view are the River Lune and Roman bathhouse, located on the rising ground above the Quay. Marsh, 22 October 2021.

2022 marked the Queen's Platinum Jubilee, and regrettably her death on 8 September 2022. A leader of immense authority and dignity, her majesty's death marked the end of an epoch. Resplendent in a tasteful Platinum Jubilee livery, Stagecoach No. 11202 is seen at the appropriately named Queen Square, Lancaster on 27 October 2022.

The transport sector has faced considerable problems retaining and attracting staff in recent years. Low pay, a lack of investment, and challenging working conditions have been cited as causes. Representing Stagecoach's recruitment programme, No. 34706, an Alexander Dennis Dart, traverses White Lund, Morecambe, on 28 October 2021.

Contrasting Stagecoach liveries at Morecambe in January 2022. No. 10030, resplendent in Ribble's post-deregulation livery, passes No. 10024, which carries a style of Stagecoach livery since superseded. The location is White Lund, a large trading estate close to the traditional boundary with Lancaster.

A trio of Stagecoach double-deckers featuring different liveries at Whitegate depot, Morecambe. By far the most interesting, No. 10030 carries the post-deregulation red used by Ribble. Nearest to the camera, No. 12207 represents the move to green power with Electric Hybrid branding. For anybody planning a visit to the depot at White Lund, it is a *very* long walk from the centre of Morecambe or Lancaster.

The leafy environs of Princes Crescent, Bare, provide an attractive background for Stagecoach No. 11209. In the background is Morecambe Bay with the prospect of Grange-over-Sands, obscured by fog and low clouds. Bare, 24 March 2022.

Resplendent in Ribble heritage livery at Morecambe is Stagecoach No. 10030. It carries a version of the short-lived but attractive post-deregulation livery, minus the slogan 'The New Ribble'. Preston-based Ribble was privatised in 1919 and purchased by Stagecoach in 1989. At one time Ribble had depots as far apart as Ambleside, Burnley, Carlisle, Liverpool, Manchester, and Skipton.

Overton has a lonely and remote atmosphere despite being close to Morecambe and Lancaster. For a brief period, Sunderland Point acted as port for Lancaster, before being superseded by Glasson on the opposite bank of the Lune. Photographed approaching Middleton is Stagecoach No. 12207. In close proximity to Overton are Heysham Power Station and the mouth of the River Lune. The area is a little reminiscent of the Isle of Grain in Kent. 17 February 2022.

Stagecoach No. 12212 carries Electric Hybrid branding at a blustery Middleton in February 2022. Stagecoach's presence in Lancashire has been much diminished in recent decades. As far back as 2001, operations in Clitheroe, East Lancashire, and Bolton were sold to the Blazefield Group, which now trades as Transdev Blazefield.

Galgate is situated in the parish of Ellel. The Lancaster Canal, M6, River Condor, and West Coast Main Line pass through the village, once famed for the production of silk. Galgate railway station closed in 1939 after just under 100 years of use. Stagecoach No. 10022, an ADL Enviro400, had just cleared Skew Bridge at Main Road when photographed on a cloudy 24 June 2022.

Kirkby Lonsdale Coach Hire (Morecambe) can be seen far and wide around Lancashire. At Glasson, Wright StreetDeck MX62 AKK was photographed on a lightly patronised run from Knott End to Lancaster. At Knott End, connections can be made with the ferry to Fleetwood. Glasson Dock was constructed in 1787 as an additional port for Lancaster. A branch of the Lancaster Canal reached Glasson in 1825, but the village never developed into a port of great significance. Glasson, 24 June 2022.

The Wyre district of Lancashire is named after the eponymous river, which enters the Irish Sea at Fleetwood. The district is bounded by Lancaster, the Ribble Valley, Preston, Blackpool, and the Fylde. At Lancaster Services on the M6 at Forton, a Mercedes-Benz Sprinter/Noone Turas combination, loads with diesel for a run north of the border. It was operated by SHM Travel of Ayrshire.

Scania N230UD/Enviro400, No. 15682 carries the latest and probably the most attractive Stagecoach corporate livery so far. It was photographed on a humid 17 August 2021 at Cabus, Lancashire, bound for Preston. On the Lancaster Canal at nearby Garstang, Rennie constructed an aqueduct over the River Wyre in 1793.

St Michael's on Wyre is a picturesque village on the route from Garstang to Fleetwood. ADL Enviro400 No. 15818 works through the village on a sultry 4 August 2021 bound for Lancaster. Stagecoach services in an area bounded roughly by Carlisle and Chorley have been marketed as Stagecoach Cumbria & North Lancashire since 2011.

Blackpool Transport No. 222 conveys a stylish and progressive image to potential bus travellers at Great Eccleston – a far cry from the plain cream AEC Swifts used in the 1970s. Nevertheless, the yellow stripes of ADL Enviro200MMC have a slight retro feel. Service 74 connects Fleetwood with Preston via Thornton and Lea.

The ADL Enviro400 City buses used by Blackpool Transport are stylish but slightly aggressive-looking machines. No.455 calls at Preesall on the east bank of the River Wyre on 24 June 2022. Blackpool Transport was founded in 1885 and rebranded as Metro Coastlines in 2001. The name Blackpool Transport was revived in 2010 and buses now carry a very smart yellow and grey colour scheme, which can be seen around the Fylde coast.

Closest to the camera at St Chad's, Poulton-le-Fylde, is Enviro400 City No. 429, working service 2 to Blackpool. No. 436 brings up the rear. Both buses carry the flagship Palladium branding. Blackpool Transport still operates trams – mostly adorned in a modern purple and white livery. Several other British towns have returned to trams, including Birmingham, Croydon, and Sheffield.

A profile photograph of an unidentified Blackpool Transport Enviro400 City at Thornton. In the background is a preserved windmill from 1794, reckoned by Nikolaus Pevsner to be the best-preserved windmill in Lancashire. Thornton, 4 August 2021.

Front and rear views of Blackpool Transport double-deckers at Fleetwood. Service 1 connects the popular Affinity Outlet at Fleetwood with Starr Gate, Blackpool. Enviro400 City No. 424, nearest the camera, traverses the tram lines on Lord Street past Enviro400 City No. 422. Ribble had depots on the Fylde at Fleetwood until 2016 and two at Blackpool until 1987–88.

Blackpool became a unitary authority on 1 April 1998 and is therefore officially outside the influence of Lancashire County Council. Pictured on the edge of the town at Mereside is this fine Mercedes-Benz 0.295 Citaro, No. 558. Service 3 connects Mereside Tesco with Bispham and Cleveleys. Mereside, 25 June 2022.

The disused Little Marton Windmill, opened in 1838, provides an echo of a more rustic era around the Fylde. Although Blackpool had a railway station by 1846, the town's growth did not accelerate until later in the century. Blackpool Transport's Mercedes-Benz Citaro No. 557 edges closer to the Mereside terminus on 25 June 2022.

Preston Bus operates service 76 between Blackpool, Weeton, Kirkham, and Lytham on the Fylde plain. At St George's Road, Optare Solo No. 20797 prepares to enter Clifton Drive, St Anne's. Preston Bus dates back to 1904 when it was known as Preston District Travel. In 1993, it was subject to a management buyout, and subsequently sold to Stagecoach in January 2009 following a period of intense competition. Stagecoach was ordered to sell Preston Bus in 2009, and since January 2011 the company has been owned by Rotala plc, Birmingham.

Both Stagecoach and Blackpool Transport penetrate the desirable Flyde resorts. At Clifton Drive, St Anne's Enviro400 City No. 420 pulls out behind No. 457 on 25 June 2022. The now defunct Fylde Borough Transport, the successor of Lytham St Anne's Corporation Transport, was noted for operating a smart, somewhat upmarket fleet of buses, in keeping with the high status of this affluent part of Lancashire.

A grab shot at Lytham illustrating Stagecoach No. 15566 in Ribble Timesaver heritage livery. A Scania N230UD/ADL Enviro400 combination, it was working towards Blackpool. Lytham is usually reckoned to be the most desirable of the Fylde seaside resorts, the genteel atmosphere a stark contrast with the brashness of Blackpool. The town merged with St Anne's, a Victorian planned town, in 1922.

Preston Bus operates several rural services located within the city boundary. At Goosnargh Lane, Goosnargh, Wright StreetLite No. 20189 works towards the city on 29 October 2021. Goosnargh was part of Preston Rural District between 1894 and 1974; the village is split between two parishes – Goosnargh and Whittingham.

The Wright StreetDeck is not the most aesthetically pleasing of bus designs. Perhaps proving the point, Preston Bus No. 40808 was seen at Sharoe Green Lane, Fulwood, in October 2021. Fulwood has a distinct identity and was independent of Preston until 1974.

On a scorching 17 July 2021, Stagecoach No. 15906 makes a sharp turn into Tithebarn Street, Preston. It carries WiFi branding, complete with appropriate imagery. A city with a long and interesting history, Domesday Book records Preston as 'Prestune' in 1086.

Preston Bus, owned by Rotala, the successor to the former municipal operator, is the principal provider of bus services in the city. Looking tired and forlorn, Nos 40411 and 40030 were photographed at Deepdale depot. The former is an East Lancs-bodied Scania N94UD new to Metrobus. The latter bus is a Scania CN230UD/Scania OmniCity new to Flights but arriving via Rotala Wessex.

A quintet of buses at Deepdale depot on 24 September 2021. The only bus springing to life is No. 40627, a Wright-bodied Volvo B5LH, preparing to work a school service. Deepdale depot, an interesting period piece, was regrettably demolished in July 2022.

Mercedes-Benz Citaro No. 33005 looks like it was being cannibalised for spare parts in this October 2021 view. Scania K230UB No. 30114 looks equally battered and forlorn. Expensive buses and still relatively young, it is perhaps surprising to see them lying idle.

A final picture from Deepdale depot illustrates an unidentified Optare Solo sans front hood. Wright Eclipse No. 66900, new to First Manchester, guards the rear. Preston, 29 October 2021.

Pictured on Deepdale Road, Deepdale is this rather fussy-looking Scania Omnilink, No. 30118. It was working the frequent Preston Bus service 6 to Red Scar, an industrial area to the east of the M6. Preston was awarded city status in 2002 and is the principal economic centre of Lancashire.

Stagecoach Scania N250UD No. 15305 is seen at Farringdon Park with Stagecoach and Ribble branding. The full title is 'Stagecoach and Ribble proud to serve Lancashire since 1919'. Carrying the Enviro 400MMC body, it was pictured at New Hall Lane, Preston, during heavy rain. Farringdon Park, 29 October 2021.

The Preston & Longridge Railway closed to passengers in 1930 and commerce in 1967, although sections to Red Scar and Deepdale survived until relatively recently. Bus travel was blamed for the decline in patronage. Traversing Ribbleton Avenue is a lightly loaded Stagecoach Enviro400 No. 15473, seen under a muggy early evening sky en route to Longridge. Ribbleton, 4 September 2021.

Preston Bus No. 40510, a Volvo B9TL/Wright Eclipse combination, swings into the Moor Nook estate. Preston is twinned with Almelo, Kalisz, Nimes and Recklinghausen. In 2015, the St Ignatius Roman Catholic Church, Preston became the Syro-Malabar Cathedral of St Alphonsa.

Near the Gamull Lane terminus at Ribbleton, Stagecoach No. 15565, a Scania N230UD, calls at Longridge Road. It was working service 1 from Longridge to Preston, which includes leafy villages such as Grimsargh, modern industrial estates at Red Scar, and densely populated inner-city terrain at Ribbleton Lane. 29 October 2021.

The headquarters of Ribble were for many years based at Frenchwood, to the south of Preston city centre. Much of the complex has been redeveloped, although a depot is retained by Stagecoach. No. 10534, resplendent in British Legion colours, stands proudly at Frenchwood on 29 October 2021.

With all the fuel stations at Gisburn and Clitheroe bereft of petrol, it was perhaps safest to travel by bus on the morning of 1 October 2021. Working its way out of Clitheroe, Mainline-branded No. 268 heads towards industrial Burnley after a torrent of rain and chaos at the fuel pumps. Clitheroe is one of the few Lancashire settlements to have an almost-complete castle. The castle stands on a rocky premonitory above the town. Construction began in Norman times, although the keep is surprisingly small.

An unexpected find at Clitheroe was this 1967 Daimler CVG6/Roe combination. New to Northampton Corporation, it now works as a bar for the Bowland Brewery of Clitheroe. Taken 1 October 2021.

Pilkington's buses can be seen far and wide in an area radiating from their base in Accrington. Pictured at Barrow, between Clitheroe and Whalley, was R20 PLK, new to Lothian. It is a Plaxton-bodied Dennis Trident, originally registered SN51 AXY. Barrow, 21 October 2021.

Ribchester has a history going back to at least Roman times when it was known as 'Bremetennacum'. Situated on the River Ribble, this pretty village stands at the junction of two Roman roads and the aforementioned fort. Photographed at Blackburn Road on the service from Wilpshire to St Celia's RC School, Longridge, it is an Alexander-bodied Dennis Trident. Owned by Longridge Coaches, it was new to East London but carries Travel De Courcey livery. The latter owner, based at Baginton, Warwickshire, ceased operating in August 2020.

Sabden is situated in the valley of the Sabden Brook, hemmed in by the Nick of Pendle and the Forest of Pendle. With a distinctly rural feel, it easy to forget that Accrington, Blackburn, Burnley, and Nelson are so close. Ribble Country's Mellor-bodied Mercedes-Benz Sprinter works out to Burnley at Padiham Road, Sabden, on 21 October 2021.

A side profile view of Pilkington's East Lancs-bodied DAF DB250 at Mire Ash Brow, Mellor. It was working a school service from Clitheroe to Mellor Brook via Langho, through picturesque countryside to the north of Blackburn. Near journey's end, it was photographed turning onto a deceptively quiet Preston New Road on 24 September 2021.

Hodsons Coaches of Clitheroe operate a school bus service for Lancashire County Council between Sawley and Rimington. Caught up in teatime traffic, Mercedes-Benz Sprinter YN09 LML was photographed in Gisburn. Until 1974 Gisburn was a Yorkshire village; it is now in the Ribble Valley district of Lancashire.

Barnoldswick is a West Riding town, which to the chagrin of its residents, was moved into the then new Pendle district of Lancashire in 1974. Within easy reach of the Forest of Bowland and Yorkshire Dales National Park, the town, pronounced 'Baa-lik', is surrounded by beautiful scenery. Pilkington's of Accrington was operating the town service on 1 October 2021 with Optare Solo YJ60 KFP.

Foulridge is situated in the Pendle district of Lancashire and within easy reach of Clitheroe, Colne, and Skipton. The village is situated on the Leeds & Liverpool Canal, which includes the Foulridge Tunnel. Construction or the tunnel began in 1792 and was completed five years later. A Mainline-branded Optare Versa calls at Skipton New Road, Foulridge, during October 2021.

Lancashire County Council operates a fleet of special buses under the name Travelcare. The department provides specialised transport services for people with disabilities and sensory impairments. There are also services for the elderly plus a dial-a-ride service in rural Flyde and Wyre. No. 40791 is a Fiat Ducato, photographed at Barrowford Road, Fence, on 1 October 2021.

The prosperous village of Higham has plenty of quaint stone-built cottages and fine views of Brierfield and Nelson. Ribble Country's Mellor-bodied Mercedes-Benz Sprinter works through Higham Hall Road, bound for nearby Burnley on 21 October 2021.

Colne town centre rests upon hilly ground above Colne Water, close to two famous Lancashire summits: Pendle Hill and the less famous Boulsworth Hill. C&S Coaches operate this Mercedes-Benz Sprinter new in 2008; it was photographed at a chilly Market Street during October 2021.

'Ey up cocker' proclaims this Ribble Country Mercedes-Benz Sprinter/Mellor combination at Colne. The passage of the bus was stopped by an inappropriately parked Audi. The much-mourned railway link between Colne and Skipton, via Earby, was severed in February 1970. Colne, 21 October 2021.

With the dramatic heights of Pendle Hill in the background, Transdev's Mainline-branded No. 271 was pictured as it approached Lane House Lane, Trawden. Close to Trawden is the scenic Wycoller Country Park and Boulsworth Hill. Hebden Bridge in West Yorkshire can be reached by crossing the Pennine Moors. Trawden, 1 October 2021.

Transdev's Wright-bodied Volvo B10BLE, No. 1091, crosses the Leeds and Liverpool Canal at Gisburn Road, Barrowford, bound for Higherford. A pretty textile village, Barrowford is situated on the Marsden (Nelson), Gisburn, and Long Preston turnpike, which connected the village with Settle, Kendal, and the Yorkshire Dales. Barrowford, 1 October 2021.

Burnley & Pendle was owned by two Lancashire local authorities, the latter selling out to Stagecoach in 1996, and the former in 1997. Departing Nelson bus station, Leyland National 2 No. 339 was new to National Welsh/Cymru Cenedlaethol in 1980 and joined Burnley & Pendle in 1987. Stagecoach disposed of its East Lancashire operations to Blazefield Travel in 2001. Nelson, 9 June 1998.

Transdev Optare Versa, No. 264, is heading for the West Yorkshire town of Keighley. The location is the small mill town of Brierfield, situated adjacent to the Leeds & Liverpool Canal. The opening of the M65 has helped reduce traffic on the A682 between Burnley and Colne. The Brierfield to Nelson connection was completed in 1983; Colne was finally reached in 1988. Brierfield, August 2021.

Reedley is one of a number of settlements between Burnley and Colne. In the borough of Pendle since 1974, Reedley, or Reedly Hallows as it is often known, was the administrative centre of the now defunct Burnley Rural District, which served the country area from 1894 to 1974. Photographed at Colne Road, Reedley is Mainline No. 255 on the regular M5 route.

Sadly, there are more slaves today than at any other time in history. Drawing attention to this injustice at Padiham is this Dennis Trident/Plaxton President, branded The Freedom Bus. Operated by Moving People of Oswaldtwistle, it was new to Lothian in June 2000. Padiham, 21 October 2021.

Despite Burnley's relatively close proximity to Leyland, the defunct municipal operator Burnley & Pendle purchased very few Leyland badged buses from 1974. No. 1313 is a Volvo B10M-50/Alexander combination, photographed in Stagecoach ownership at Burnley during 1998. It was working service 21 to the small town of Padiham.

Climbing up Manchester Road, Hapton is Mainline-branded Optare Versa, No. 249. All trace of Hapton Castle has disappeared but the architecturally noteworthy Shuttleworth Hall of 1639 remains in use. Huncoat and Padiham power stations, which closed in 1984 and 1993 respectively, were located near Hapton.

Resplendent in the latest Witchway colour scheme is this sleek-looking ADL Enviro400 MMC. Transdev's flagship X43 service connects Burnley with Rawtenstall, Prestwich, and Manchester. Some early morning services depart from Nelson. Pictured at Dunnockshaw, above Burnley, is No. 2004, surrounded by a typically bleak West Pennine background.

Altham is a village in the northern part of Hyndburn, a borough based principally around the town of Accrington. Despite the rural-looking setting, industry is never too far away, the large Altham Industrial Estate overshadowing the village. Transdev's No. 2768 works the company's flagship Hotline-branded route 152, between Burnley and Preston at Syke Side on 21 October 2021.

Great Harwood is typical of the mill towns around Accrington. Smallish in size with long rows of terraced housing, and verdant green hills always within view of the town centre. Working out to Blackburn is No. 1700, a Wright-bodied Volvo B7RLE, part of the Blackburn Bus Company fleet. The location is Blackburn Road, Great Harwood, with the town hall in the background.

The west side of Accrington town centre is dominated by this graceful viaduct built in 1847. The development of railways in the Hyndburn area posed several engineering challenges due to the hilly topography of the West Pennine Moors. Transdev No. 285, an Optare Versa, departs the modern bus station on 1 August 2021.

Also at Accrington is Transdev No. 283, attired in 464 branding for the scenic run to Rochdale via Bacup. Famous people associated with Accrington include Jon Anderson, lead singer of Yes, and First World War veteran Netherwood Hughes. Accrington, 1 August 2021.

A third shot from Accrington illustrates Transdev No. 253, attired in Mainline livery. Mills, coal and bricks made Accrington prosperous. Despite the production of red bricks known as 'Accrington bloods', a tour around the town will reveal most buildings to be built of stone.

Passing through Rishton is No. 100 of the Blackburn Bus Co. It is a Volvo B7TL attired in a special livery commemorating the Ribble Motor Services Centenary. Note the registration R100 TDV, a reference to owner Transdev. Rishton is one of the smaller Lancashire textile towns, situated between Blackburn and Clayton-le-Moors.

High above Blackburn is the suburb of Beardwood, situated close to the dramatic heights above Witton Country Park. At Preston New Road, Stagecoach No. 15567 collects a young couple on route 59 to the Royal Blackburn Hospital. The borough of Blackburn with Darwen became a unitary authority on 1 April 1998.

Turning from Primrose Bank onto Larkhill on the A666 is this colourful Optare Versa in service with Blackburn Private Hire. The tower blocks represent the post-war redevelopment of Daisyfield. Close by are the sloping terraced streets of Whalley Range and Brookhouse, home to a predominantly Muslim population. Daisyfield, 29 October 2021.

An archive photograph from 11 August 2000 showing Blackburn's Leyland National Greenway No. 521. It had been new to Ribble in 1981 as LFR855X, and came via London & Country in 1992. The Greenway was constructed by East Lancs as an attempt to modernise the sturdy Leyland National body. No. 521 was pictured amid ugly post-war architecture at Ainsworth Street, Blackburn, bound for Higher Croft.

Blackburn Private Hire's Optare Solo YJ62 FHU is pictured on service 10, a circular linking the town to Revidge and Lammack. Photographed at Wensley Road, Wensley Fold, YJ62 FHU is seen amid hilly terraced streets, typical of Blackburn and the surrounding towns. Famous people associated with Blackburn include Gladstone's biographer Lord Morley, actor Ian McShane, and businessman Zuber Vali Issa. Wensley Fold, 15 September 2021.

The minarets of the Masjide Noorul Islam (Mosque) rise like candlesticks above terraced housing at Audley Range, Blackburn. The town has a significant Muslim population, along with several mosques and masjids. Moving People operate this Optare Solo YJO4 CCW, named *Jessica*. It was photographed on service 33 to central Blackburn on 24 September 2021.

Moving People were also operating this elderly Plaxton-bodied Dennis Dart, named *Graham*, on the weekday service to Darwen. The location is North Road, Queen's Park. The notorious Queen's Park flats were demolished by Blackburn with Darwen Council on 13 January 2002, following the successful clearance of Mill Hill flats in 2000.

Hotline branding is appropriate on a freezing and foggy Saturday morning at Burnley Road, Blackburn. Wright-bodied Volvo B9TL, No. 2772, works the trunk route 152 to Burnley in absolutely dismal conditions at Whitebirk. Blackburn, 18 December 2021.

Hoddlesden is a pretty West Pennine village a few miles from Darwen and once served by Blackburn Transport (and the earlier Darwen Corporation). Carus Mill, a local landmark, was destroyed by fire in 2008 and has been demolished. Despite the proximity to Blackburn and Darwen, bus services are infrequent. Harris Travel was using this Alexander-bodied Dennis Trident on a school run from Waterloo (St Bede) to Guide. Approaching Queen Street, LX03 NGZ was new to Stagecoach London. Hoddlesden, 23 June 2022.

Service 152 between Preston and Burnley passes through industrial towns and charming countryside. Transdev No. 2766 had just cleared the Boars Head, Hoghton, on a clammy 23 June 2022. Hoghton Tower is a mansion and popular attraction. It was visited by James I in 1617.

A second picture from the Chorley district of Lancashire illustrates Transdev No. 2754, a Wright-bodied Volvo B7TL. It was turning into Dole Lane, Abbey Village, on a sweltering 23 June 2022, six years after the Brexit plebiscite. Abbey Village shows some evidence of being a planned industrial community, although it was connected with the ruined, much older Whalley Abbey.

Rising Bridge is situated in the borough of Rossendale but carries an Accrington postcode. With typical West Pennine scenery, Optare Versa No. 237 heads north towards Accrington at Blackburn Road on 4 September 2021.

The cobbled, rain-soaked road and sober stone buildings add a touch of atmosphere to this shot of Optare Solo No. 162 at Haslingden. Carrying Transdevs Rossendale Rovers branding, it was pictured working out to Rawtenstall on a dismal day in September 2021.

The Blackburn Bus Company operates the X41 between Accrington and Manchester. Photographed on the Rossendale section, No. 1868 in Red Express branding works through a humid Haslingden. The Irish nationalist and republican Michael Davitt spent many years in Haslingden. He died in Dublin on 30 May 1906, aged sixty.

The charmingly named Love Clough in Rossendale is the location for Witchway branded No. 2013, an ADL Enviro400 MMC. Fitted with Wi-Fi, passengers should skip the internet and admire the beautiful but rugged countryside. Love Clough, June 2022.

Another striking Transdev livery is carried by No. 1730, in Irwell Line branding at Waterfoot. A Wright-bodied Volvo B7RLE, it is based at the former Blackburn Transport depot at Intack. Route 483 connects Bury with Burnley, following part of the River Irwell. The River Irwell rises at Deerplay Moor, a few miles above Bacup. Waterfoot, 23 June 2022.

The villages in Rossendale district are noted for their unique names. Some of the most intriguing include Brittania, Crawshawbooth, Goodshaw, Higher Change, and Laund. At Stacksteads, Transdev's Optare Versa No. 289 departs Newchurch Road for Rochdale. Stacksteads, 23 June 2022.

A painfully humid Bacup sees Transdev No. 283 on service 464 to Rochdale, Greater Manchester. The 1980s BBC television series *Juliet Bravo* was filmed around East Lancashire, including Bacup and Rawtenstall. Bacup, 23 June 2022.

Almost but not quite in Greater Manchester, Transdev No. 1864, based at Intack, is seen in typical Rossendale surroundings at Stubbins. A Wright-bodied Volvo B7RLE, it was working the X41 to Manchester.

Westhoughton was the home town of the late Robert Shaw, noted for his memorable performances in *From Russia With Love* (1963), *The Sting* (1973), and *Jaws* (1975). Shaw died in 1978 during the making of *Avalanche Express* (1979), his voice being dubbed by a mimic. Working out to Bolton at dusk is Stagecoach No. 19517, an ADL Enviro400. Westhoughton, December 2021.

Amid rather sober-looking architecture, First Manchester No. 3083, a Leyland Olympian/ Northern Counties combination, passes through Bolton bound for Withins, an area east of Bolton town centre in the Breightmet area. People associated with Bolton include Andrew Longworth, Samuel Crompton, and Annie Haslam. Films made in Bolton include *The Family Way* (1966) and *Spring and Port Wine* (1969). Both capture the industrial atmosphere of the town perfectly.

Bradshawgate is one of the key routes into central Bolton. Once a busy shopping street, by 2022 the area was looking sadly dilapidated and impoverished. Diamond No. 40736 was photographed amid urban decay en route to Bury on 14 October 2022.

First Greater Manchester still operated service 37 between Manchester and Bolton on 30 June 2019. Bolton depot was acquired by Rotala (Diamond Bus North West) on 11 August 2019. Cheetham Hill depot had already passed to Go-Ahead's, new Go North West subsidiary on 2 June 2019. First No. 33730 was pictured working along Bolton Road, Farnworth, bound for Bolton.

First Greater Manchester No. 33673 has just passed underneath the busy A666 at Moses Gate between Bolton and Farnworth. First services within Greater Manchester are now focused primarily on Manchester, Oldham, and Rochdale. Vantage services are operated from Bolton in a garage shared with Arriva. Moses Gate, June 2019.

During the planning of Greater Manchester metropolitan county it was proposed to place Bury within an enlarged Rochdale borough. To the relief of Bury, the idea was shelved and the town instead became a metropolitan borough, absorbing Prestwich, Ramsbottom, and Whitefield. On 27 April 2002, Leyland Olympian/Northern Counties No. 3101 departs Bury for Rochdale on service 471.

Early morning on a rain-drenched 26 November 2021. Before rush-hour traffic has started at Heywood, Go North West No. 3250 was pictured patiently waiting customers for Manchester. Heywood is situated between Bury and Rochdale, being administered by the latter borough since 1974.

Rossendale developed a significant presence in the Rochdale area following deregulation in 1986. Photographed at the now demolished Rochdale bus station is No. 72, a 1987 Volvo B10M-61/Duple Dominant combination that came via Alexander, Milngavie in 1997.

Situated on the edge of Greater Manchester, close to Rochdale, is the small town of Littleborough. Photographed leaving the railway station is First Greater Manchester No. 63107, a Wrightbus Streetlite. Points of interest near Littleborough include Blackstone Edge and Hollingworth Lake. The local scenery is a mixture of the bleak, desolate, foreboding, and spectacular. Littleborough, March 2019.

At the break of dawn on a damp 26 November 2021, First Greater Manchester No. 33744 stands empty at Royton bound for Rochdale. Passenger numbers fell dramatically following the pandemic and have yet to return to normal levels.

Bright sunshine provides a distraction for the driver of First Greater Manchester No. 33675, an ADL Enviro400, at Royton on 25 March 2022. Royton is part of the Oldham district of Greater Manchester.

On the rural-urban fringe of Oldham is the community of Grotton. At the bus terminus, a fine Wright-bodied Volvo B9TL, No. 37456, prepares to work downhill to Manchester. Grotton was actually a West Riding settlement until 1974.

At Lees Road, Oldham, First No.37430 was pictured working service 84 to Uppermill. The Saddleworth division of the West Riding was placed into Oldham metropolitan district in 1974.

Leaving the village of Lees and about to enter Oldham is First Greater Manchester No. 37383. The background is typical of the Oldham area: large, rather severe brick mills – in this case Leesbrook Mill, a Grade II listed building.

Failsworth is situated between Manchester and Oldham along the busy A62. Despite much redevelopment there are a few signs of the older town to be found near Failsworth Pole. Failsworth attracts visitors to its antique quarter around Wrigley Head. Working the A62 into Manchester is First No.33676 on a crisp 26 November 2021.

Droylsden forms part of the metropolitan borough of Tameside, a district comprising a number of towns annexed from both Lancashire and Cheshire in 1974. Ashton, Mossley, and Droylsden shown in this publication represent the Lancashire side. Stagecoach No. 10598 collects passengers near Edge Lane, bound for Ashton-under-Lyne on a stormy 26 November 2022.

A rear-view picture of Stagecoach No. 10598 at Manchester Road, Droylsden. Visible are the Pennines and the tramlines linking Manchester with Ashton-under-Lyne. A Moravian settlement was established at Fairfield, Droyslden, by Benjamin Latrobe in 1785. A theological seminary opened in 1875 but closed in 1958.

A sign of the times at the marketplace, Ashton-under-Lyne. Holmeswood provided this coach for NHS Covid-19 vaccinations in Tameside. A mixed group of people queue up patiently to enter 0Y21 CCD, a MAN/Mobipeople Explorer on 26 November 2021.

Mossley is high up in the moorlands of the upper Tame Valley, just in historic Lancashire. The Pennines and Saddleworth Moor provide a stunning backdrop. Before the creation of SELNEC in 1969, the forerunner of Greater Manchester PTE, transport in the area was provided by the SHMD. This commenced in 1904 and was a joint venture between four councils, bearing the unwieldy name of Stalybridge, Hyde, Mossley & Dukinfield Tramways & Electricity Board. Stotts, Optare Solo approaches Mossley in November 2021.

Great swathes of Collyhurst, Manchester, have been swept away leaving bare spaces, some of which are now being used to build 'affordable housing'. Traversing Rochdale Road, this angular-looking Stagecoach Enviro400 was pictured working service 119 between Higher Blackley and Piccadilly. In an interesting development, Transport for Greater Manchester provided free bus travel for Ukrainian refugees for 48 hours on arrival in the metropolitan boroughs during 2022.

Impressive beasts with a distinct presence are the Plaxton Elite-bodied Volvo B11RT, used by Megabus. Stagecoach Megabus was formed in 2003 as low-cost coach operator. In 2012, services expanded to mainland Europe, but these were sold to Flixbus (Germany) in 2016. During December 2021, Megabus passed to ComfortDelGro. No. 54283 draws close to central Manchester at Rochdale Road, Newtown, on 25 March 2022.

A dismal Saturday morning at Cheetham Hill Road, Cheetham, with Go North West No. 3251, heading north towards Bury. Manchester's ever-changing skyline forms the backdrop in December 2021. The IRA bombing of Manchester in 1996 has, ironically, been credited with the renaissance of the city christened Cottonopolis by the Victorians.

Cheetham Hill is just north of Cheetham and Manchester city centre. Go North West No. 3226 is a Wright-bodied Volvo B9TL and was pictured heading towards the city centre at Cheetham Hill Road after a typical Manchester downpour.

An atmospheric rear-view photograph of preserved Lancashire United No. 97. New in 1962, it carries sober Northern Counties bodywork, which was constructed on an early Daimler Fleetline chassis. Lancashire United was based at Atherton, Lancashire. Formed in 1905, the company was acquired by Greater Manchester PTE in 1976 and dissolved in 1981. No. 97 presents a fine sight at Boyle Street, Manchester, in November 2021.

Deep within inner-city Manchester, Stagecoach Enviro400 works a relatively quiet Bradford Road, Holt Town, on 26 November 2021. Service 76 connects Oldham Mumps with Manchester via Limeside, Hollinwood, Failsworth, and Miles Platting. The former industrial community of Holt Town was founded by David Holt in 1785. Like much of inner Manchester, the area has been reconstructed, with acres of Victorian cottages swept away.

On a typically wet Manchester day, Stagecoach No. 12023 makes the gentle ascent up Briscoe Lane, Newton Heath on 12 November 2021. In the distance are the now iconic gas holders at Bradford.

Harpurhey is a much-rebuilt suburb of inner Manchester. Rows and rows of traditional Manchester brick cottages have been swept away and replaced with more modern housing. Working towards central Manchester, First No. 37412 was photographed at Fernclough Road, near Rochdale Road. Harpurhey, 25 March 2022.

Transport for Greater Manchester coordinates a free bus service around the centre of Manchester. Using diesel-electric power, Optare Versa No. 49102 works service 2, a circular connecting Piccadilly, Shudehill, and Victoria.

First Manchester No. 5429 is a late MCW Metrobus, new in 1989 to Strathclyde; it was part of a batch transferred from First Glasgow in 2001–02. It was photographed in the familiar surroundings of Oldham Street, Manchester. The controversial historian A. J. P. Taylor described Manchester as 'irredeemably ugly'. He went on to write: 'There is no spot to which you could lead a blindfold stranger and say happily: "Now open your eyes".'

On 27 April 2002, Stagecoach Manchester No. 719, an Alexander-bodied Volvo Olympian leaves Piccadilly bound for Southern Cemetery. On the right, Stagecoach Magic Bus No. 3057, an earlier Northern Counties-bodied Leyland Olympian awaits passengers for West Didsbury. 'Magic Bus' was a moderately successful single by The Who in 1968, which became a live favourite when stretched out to inordinate length in concert.

The iconic and recently restyled 'M' logo is displayed proudly on the bus stop flag at Ashton Old Road, Higher Openshaw. The Transport for Greater Manchester logo reassures anybody with poor geographical knowledge exactly which conurbation they are in. Stagecoach No. 10598 collects passengers for Manchester, despite the destination displaying Ashton. Openshaw was the birthplace of the late Davy Jones.

The spire of the Church of God of Prophecy Christian Centre is a notable landmark on Moss Lane East, Moss Side. Stagecoach No. 10044 works a mid-afternoon journey to Flixton on a day of windy and unsettled weather in November 2021.

The large Heineken UK brewery on the corner of Princess Road and Moss Lane East dominates this picture of Stagecoach ADL Enviro400 No. 19449, at Moss Side. The area, bounded by Chorlton-on-Medlock, Fallowfield, Hulme, Rusholme, and Whalley Range, has a significant ethnic population. Most of the original Moss Side has been cleared and rebuilt.

Longsight is well known for its locomotive depot and works, although the railway station closed as long ago as 1958. Photographed on the busy Stockport Road is Stagecoach No.11522, working towards central Manchester. Longsight is one of Manchester's most diverse neighbourhoods.

The busy Wilmslow Road works its way through Rusholme, an area of Manchester with a distinctly Middle Eastern vibe. Curry houses and exotic eateries have made the area popular with connoisseurs of foreign food. Displaying specialist Electric Zero Emissions branding, Stagecoach No. 14029 is an ADL Enviro400 City resplendent in a smart green environmental-themed livery.

Upper Chorlton Road forms the administrative boundary between the city of Manchester and Trafford metropolitan borough. On the Darley Park, Stretford side, in Trafford, Stagecoach ADL Enviro400 MMC, No. 10413, works towards Piccadilly on service 86 from Chorlton. Autumnal conditions prevail in this November 2021 image.

Trafford metropolitan borough contains areas previously in Cheshire, including Altrincham, Hale, and Warburton. On the Lancashire side and what might be called Manchester over the border are suburban Davyhulme, Flixton, and Urmston. Negotiating Davyhulme Circle, we see Arriva No. 2675, a Wright-bodied VDL, working to Altrincham.

Brightening up a miserable teatime rush hour at Redclyffe Road, Dumplington, is this handsome Mercedes-Benz Citaro in service with Diamond. No. 33023 is working out to Agecroft via Barton Bridge. The Manchester Ship Canal passes under Barton Road Swing Bridge, opened on 1 January 1894.

The orange paintwork on the front of Orbits-branded No. 6154 recalls Greater Manchester PTE days. It is a Wright-bodied Volvo B7RL and is en route to the gargantuan Trafford Centre. Barton-upon-Irwell, November 2021.

Go North West No. 6004, carries a poppy and MCR branding at Eccles Interchange. Bringing up the rear is Diamond's Optare Versa No. 30141. 'MCR' has become quite common as an abbreviation for Manchester. Eccles is now administered by the city of Salford.

Pendleton can claim to be the effective centre of Salford; the vast blocks of Salford Shopping City are a notable landmark for the surrounding area. Little of what L. S. Lowry painted around Pendleton survives. Electric Hybrid-branded Stagecoach No. 12045 collects passengers at Pendleton for the run to East Didsbury, Manchester, on a freezing 26 November 2021.

The Manchester Metrolink transformed public transport in Greater Manchester and breathed new life into the Bury to Victoria line. At Weaste, Bombardier M5000, No.3125, heads west towards Eccles on 25 March 2022. The Manchester Metrolink opened in 1992 and currently connects Altrincham, Bury, East Didsbury, Eccles, Manchester Airport, Oldham, Rochdale, and The Trafford Centre. There are currently ninety-nine stations, perhaps the best named being Besses o' th' Barn and Oldham Mumps.

6CCX operates for Chesters Executive Travel of Walkden. A Scania N270UD/East Lancs combination, it was new to Nottingham City Transport as YT09 YHR. Here it turns into Park Road, Walkden, on 25 November 2021.

Irlam is an industrial, or perhaps more accurately a post-industrial, town situated between Chat Moss and the River Irwell. The steel works closed in 1979 as part of British Steel's rationalisation plans; the site is now home to the Northbank Industrial Estate. Go North West No. 3237 collects passengers at Liverpool Road, Irlam, bound for Manchester.

No. 9003, a Wright-bodied Volvo B7RLE is a member of the Go North West training fleet. Having cleared the old railway line between Glazebrook East Junction and Skelton Junction (Timperley) at Cadishead Viaduct, the bus will continue to navigate the housing estates of Cadishead and Irlam.

The Leigh–Salford–Manchester Bus Rapid Transit scheme began operation on 3 April 2016 at a cost of £122 million. At Sale Lane, Tyldesley (Parr Brow), is First No. 39255 in Vantage branding. The route makes partial use of the former Tyldesley Loopline, which closed on 5 May 1969.

One of the old soldiers of the Arriva North West fleet is this 2005 VDL/Wright Cadet combination. Pictured on layover at Leigh, it was working service 34 to St Helens in Merseyside. Leigh's industrial history is based upon coal mining and textiles.

The market town of Ashton-in-Makerfield rests on the Lancashire coalfield. The collieries have closed and the lunar-like landscape of spoil heaps and lakes, known as 'flashes', have been landscaped. Arriva No. 4605 pauses in the town centre en route for St Helens during December 2021.

Warrington's Own Buses, perhaps remarkably, continues as a municipal operator in 2023. Lancashire municipals such as Blackburn, Fylde, Hyndburn, Lancaster, Rossendale, and more recently Halton, have all ceased trading. Services from Warrington penetrate as far as Altrincham, Newton-le-Willows, and Northwich. Former Metroline (London) ADL Enviro400, No. 312, departs Leigh for Warrington on 9 December 2021.

Golborne carries a Warrington postcode despite being administered by the borough of Wigan. A former mining community, the village was rocked by tragedy in 1979 when ten men died following an explosion triggered by firedamp. Another miner was seriously injured. The pit, located in an area known as 'Bonk', closed in 1989. Pictured in Golborne on 25 November 2021 is Arriva No. 2970, on service 360 to Warrington.

Almost in Greater Manchester, on Warrington's eastern fringe, is the village of Hollins Green. Located in the civil parish of Rixton-with-Glazebrook, the village was part of Cheshire between 1974 and 1998. Parked outside the Black Swan is No. 3214, surrounded by some lovely daffodils.

Warrington is both an old and a new town. The town, recorded in the Domesday Book, was granted a market in 1255 and was an important bridging point during the English Civil War. In 1967, Warrington was designated a new town for the south Lancashire region. Westbrook in north-west Warrington is typical of the town – expansive, modern suburbs – and here No. 236 loads at Asda on service 17 to Golden Square.

The cooling towers of the decommissioned Fiddler's Ferry Power Station dominate this view of Warrington's Own Buses No. 83. A Wright-bodied Volvo B7RLE, it was seen approaching Penketh, a settlement to the west of Warrington. December 2021.

In better weather conditions, Warrington's Optare Versa, No. 102, approaches Penketh with the destination incorrectly displaying 'Widnes Market'. Fiddler's Ferry Power Station was commissioned in 1971–73 and can be seen from as far away as the M62, near Milnrow.

Warrington's Own Buses No. 88 is a Volvo B7RLE with sleek Wright Eclipse Urban 2 bodywork. It was recorded at Widnes Road, Cuerdley Cross, which is almost, but not quite, in Halton. Out of shot behind the hedges is the monstrous but impressive Fiddler's Ferry Power Station, which was decommissioned on 31 March 2020. Cuerdley Cross, December 2021.

Halton district was inaugurated in 1974 and became a constituent part of the revised Cheshire county. Now a unitary authority, it includes what was historically Lancashire's most southerly point: Hale Head and the Cheshire town of Runcorn. Arriva No. 3044 approaches Hale Bank, from Hale, on a welcome stretch of green belt close to the River Mersey.

West Bank is a distinct settlement on the north bank of the River Mersey at Widnes. There are splendid views of Runcorn, Fiddler's Ferry Power Station, and the recently opened Mersey Gateway Bridge. In Preston Bus livery, Ashcroft's Optare Solo, PO56 RRV was photographed at rest on St Mary's Road during December 2021.

Widnes was once said to be England's most polluted town due to the abundance of chemical plants located around the River Mersey. On a crisp and atmospherically pure December day, Arriva No. 3023 leaves Widnes Market (Simms Cross) for Warrington. In the background No. 5003 waits for more customers.

Ashcroft Travel operates a number of services in the Widnes area. HIG8904 (GX54DWC) is an ageing but still respectable Dennis Dart SLF/Plaxton Pointer 2 combination, pictured at Widnes Market (Simms Cross). The town of Widnes was allegedly the inspiration for Paul Simon to write his classic song 'Homeward Bound'. Some revisionists have posited Warrington, Wigan, or even the now closed Ditton station, as other possible locations for the composition of the tune.

Arriva No. 3023 leaves a threatening sky behind at Widnes as it prepares to cross Queensway over the River Mersey en route for Runcorn. Halton is one of a small number of English local authorities to have territory within two historic counties; the others include Doncaster, Oldham, Richmond-upon-Thames, Sandwell, Stockton-on-Tees, and Tameside.

Arriva No. 2691 works the regular 352 route between St Helens and Wigan at Billinge. The village has the highest point in Merseyside: Billinge Hill, also known less attractively as Billinge Lump. Snowdonia, Blackpool Tower, and Manchester are visible on clear days. Billinge, 9 December 2021.

Haydock, Merseyside, was part of south Lancashire's colliery country, the last mine closing in 1971. Haydock was also the birthplace of St Edward Arrowsmith, executed in 1628 at Lancaster and canonised in October 1970. Hatton's Optare Solo MX08 MGU works towards historic Garswood at Haydock on 31 July 2021.

St Helens is famous for coal mining and the manufacture of glass. The town became a metropolitan district within Merseyside in 1974. On a gloomy 10 December 2021, Hatton's dual-door Enviro200 passes Huyton Travel's Optare Solo YD63 VCA outside the Merseytravel bus station.

Arriva has a significant presence in St Helens. Leading a quartet of Arriva buses is No. 2508, a VDL/Wright Commander combination that still looks impressive in December 2021. Arriva's antecedents included Merseyside PTE, which became operational in December 1969, with St Helens and Southport joining the executive in April 1974 on the formation of Merseyside metropolitan county.

Earlestown is the commercial centre of Newton-le-Willows. Pictured opposite the town hall of 1892, Arriva No. 2615 is a Plaxton Centro-bodied VDL DE12BSSB120. Earlestown joins Bedworth, Castleford, Nelson, and Scunthorpe as a target for Nikolaus Pevsner's acid pen, the architecture expert describing the town in 1969 as 'having nothing to recommend it, except perhaps the station...'

Warrington's Own Buses reach several contrasting destinations outside the borough, including Northwich, and Warburton. At Newton-le-Willows, Wright-bodied DAF SB120 No. 76 works towards Warrington on 16 December 2021.

Prescot is situated in the Knowsley district of Merseyside, between Huyton and St Helens. Cumfybus were using this rather anonymous-looking Optare Solo on service 239 between Prescot and Broadgreen on 10 December 2021. A few Georgian buildings survive in Prescot, a town famous for the manufacture of clocks, watches and later cables.

Halewood and nearby Speke are famous for their association with the motor industry. Triumph had a notorious, strike-prone plant at Speke producing the ill-fated TR7. Ford assembled the Capri and Escort for many years at Halewood with less unrest. Working along Leather's Lane, Halewood, is Arriva No. 4475, a Wright Eclipse Gemini 2. The Jaguar Land Rover plant is in the distance. Halewood, 9 December 2021.

Kirkby is a large post-war development, often reckoned to be a part of Liverpool, but actually in the metropolitan borough of Knowsley. Idling at the modern bus station is Hatton's ADL Enviro200, No. 131 on route 297 to St Helens.

Kirkby's large Northwood estate is the location for Stagecoach No. 10565. Perhaps carrying too much information for potential passengers, it is seen on the final leg of the journey before returning to Liverpool. My ride on service 217 revealed willingness from passengers to use the Wi-Fi, but not their face coverings! Northwood, December 2021.

Having a break from driver-training duties at Hunts Cross is Arriva No. 8260, a Volvo B7RLE/Wright Eclipse Urban, based at Speke depot. It was previously owned by KMP, Llanberis, Gwynedd.

Resplendent in driver training livery is Arriva No. 8300 at Western Avenue, Speke. It is an Alexander-bodied Volvo B7TL, new in 2006 and based at Speke depot. Both George Harrison and Paul McCartney lived briefly in Speke.

Representing the Stagecoach presence within the city of Liverpool is No. 15581, a Scania N230UD/ADL Enviro400 combination. Stagecoach Merseyside & South Lancashire are based at Gillmoss depot, Liverpool, and reach destinations as diverse as Chester, Chorley, Runcorn, Southport, and Wrexham. Garston, August 2021.

Well over fifty buildings were destroyed in the Lodge Lane area of Liverpool in July 1981 as a result of the Toxteth riots. On 9 December 2021, Arriva No. 4669 traverses a peaceful and multicultural Lodge Lane, Toxteth, on the Sheil Road Circular.

A rear view of former Merseyside PTE Alexander-bodied Leyland Atlantean, one of a small number of Atlanteans to receive B-registration plates. New in August 1984, it was in fact the last Atlantean to be delivered to the PTE. Now preserved in MTL livery, it was originally based on the Wirral Peninsula, a part of Merseyside annexed from Cheshire in 1974. The location is Boyle Street, Manchester.

Queen Square has replaced the old Hood Street gyratory as a key Liverpool transport hub. Leading a procession of Arriva buses is No. 5002, a MAN EcoCity with Caetano bodywork at dusk on 10 December 2021. Famous people from Liverpool include William Gladstone, John Lennon, Kim Catrall, Billy Fury, and the legendary Richard Starkey (Ringo Starr).

Arriva No. 4801 is a Wright-bodied Volvo B5LH, resplendent in Electric Hybrid branding. It was pictured on one of December 2021's grimiest days at Callestock Close, Croxteth, bound for Liverpool city centre.

Bootle is a town in its own right and not just a northern suburb of Liverpool. Located in Sefton district, Bootle was once a resort before the arrival of industry and the docks. Pictured at the greatly redeveloped New Strand are a trio of Arriva buses, with No. 4827 closest to the camera. Bootle, 9 December 2021.

Penny Lane is one of the most famous suburban streets in Liverpool due to the Beatles' 1967 double A-side single 'Penny Lane'/'Strawberry Fields Forever'. Both songs reflect the different world view of the Beatles' principal writers – McCartney's optimism and Lennon's introspection. Leaving Bootle for Penny Lane is Arriva No. 4694, an ADL Enviro400 MMC, photographed on 10 December 2021.

Working towards Aigburth Vale in Liverpool, Arriva No. 3047 was pictured at Marsh Lane, Bootle, surrounded by a mixture of architectural styles. A DAF SB200/Wright combination, it had previously carried gold Investors in People livery.

North of Bootle is the seaside town of Crosby, sometimes explicitly differentiated as Waterloo and Great Crosby. At the Waterloo end, named after the Napoleonic battle of 1815, stands Arriva No. 3022. A typical Wright-bodied VDL DE02FSSB200. Sefton metropolitan district is a long, thin borough stretching up the coast from Bootle to Southport, almost at the mouth of the River Ribble.

Ormskirk is situated between the Merseyside conurbation and Preston in a flat landscape administered by West Lancashire Borough Council. Scania N230UD/ADL Enviro400 No. 15854 carries Stagecoach Gold branding – a luxury brand intended to attract middle-class passengers. It came via Stagecoach West's Gloucester depot. Reports suggest Stagecoach intend to disband the Gold scheme.

Skelmersdale was designated a new town in 1961. With a population of approximately 40,000, 'Skem' is one of the biggest towns without a railway station in England – Dudley, Newcastle-under-Lyme, and Washington are others. The station on the Rainford Junction to Ormskirk line closed to the public in 1956, before final demolition in 1968. At the BP fuel station on Railway Road, Newtown, are a trio of Mercedes-Benz Sprinters in service with Lancashire County Council.

A final shot, taken early on a December morning, in atrociously thick fog at Shadsworth. Blackburn's No. 1061, a Volvo B10BLE/Wright Renown, prepares to leave Fecitt Brow for a challenging journey to Clitheroe in the Ribble Valley. Shadsworth, December 2021.